Charles Coolidge Read

The Insurance of Children

Charles Coolidge Read

The Insurance of Children

ISBN/EAN: 9783744723787

Printed in Europe, USA, Canada, Australia, Japan

Cover: Foto ©ninafisch / pixelio.de

More available books at **www.hansebooks.com**

THE INSURANCE OF CHILDREN.

ARGUMENT OF

CHARLES COOLIDGE READ

BEFORE THE

COMMITTEE ON INSURANCE

OF THE

MASSACHUSETTS LEGISLATURE,

APRIL 4, 1895,

IN BEHALF OF THE BILL TO

PROHIBIT THE INSURANCE OF CHILDREN UNDER TEN YEARS OF AGE.

AMENDED COPY OF STENOGRAPHIC REPORT.

BOSTON:
ALFRED MUDGE & SON, PRINTERS,
No. 24 FRANKLIN STREET.
1895.

COMMITTEE ON INSURANCE.

EDWARD B. ATWOOD, OF PLYMOUTH COUNTY,
GEORGE L. GAGE, OF ESSEX COUNTY,
JOSEPH B. MACCABE, OF SUFFOLK COUNTY,

On the part of the Senate.

JOHN L. BATES, OF BOSTON,
J. EDWARD HOLLIS, OF NEWTON,
J. FRANK PORTER, OF DANVERS,
CHARLES L. YOUNG, OF SPRINGFIELD,
JOHN C. SPOFFORD, OF EVERETT,
MICHAEL W. COLLINS, OF BOSTON,
WILLIAM W. DAVIS, OF BOSTON,
THOMAS F. HOBAN, OF LOWELL,

On the part of the House.

CLOSING ARGUMENT OF CHARLES COOLIDGE READ, IN BEHALF OF PETITIONERS.

Mr. Chairman and Gentlemen: One of Governor Long's last sentences, which he delivered in his most impressive manner, was this: "For God's sake, don't let this child be buried in a pauper's grave!" and I reply to Governor Long, representing, as I do, the charitable men and women from one end of this Commonwealth to the other, "For God's sake, don't let this *living child be starved* and neglected while it is *alive*, through this wrongful child life insurance!" The governor is taking care of the child after it is *dead!* The ladies and gentlemen who are with me are hoping that you will help us to take care of the child while it is yet *alive*, and not delay until its poor little body is prepared to be laid away in the grave. And, right here, I wish, from the volumes of evidence that have been taken at these hearings, to read to you a sentence from a gentleman who is respected in this city, and in Cambridge, and throughout the Commonwealth, the Rev. Mr. Beach, of Cambridge. You will remember it; it is pertinent to the governor's remark: "Finally, I should think the facts in this case, as they have been brought out by experts, ought to touch the hardest hearts. I should think the existence of the great companies such as we have had named before us, with their enormous properties and their great buildings, going around through their runners and getting the money away from these poor people, so that a family of children has to live on a can of condensed milk a week, — I should think that they would go to their next directors' meeting, and vote themselves to take no more such insurance as that. It seems as if in these times the one scheme was not to get money by actual service, not to give an honest equivalent for the thing that is bartered or the thing that is produced, but it seems as if the scheme were to get something for nothing, to invent means to get something for nothing; as if a plutocracy were abroad in the world, trying to make itself rich, and to feather its own nest at the cost of the blood and tears and deaths of human beings.

"I believe, gentlemen of this committee, we have got to call a halt; we have got to make some protection to the poor and to the little children; we have got to put a mark, and say, 'Beyond that thou shalt not go, oh, thou money power.'"

And let me quote also a sentence from the remarks of the eloquent gentleman who was here the day before yesterday, Mr. Edward Atkinson: "Bearing in mind that upon you rests the honor of the State of Massachusetts, — and if I were a judge charging you as a jury, what I would say to you would be this; 'If there is a doubt, give it for life, not for death,' — if there is a doubt in your minds that by licensing child insurance of tender years, you may promote death, notwithstanding the incidental benefit, notwithstanding all that may be put before you of what has been gained, the gain is not worth the death of one single infant; and you who hold the honor of Massachusetts in your custody will see that you do not give warrant for the neglect of the feeble and the helpless, or the death of an infant."

Gentlemen, we have all listened with pleasure to the remarks of Governor Long. It is always a pleasure to hear him speak, because of his rare gift of language and his great power of argument; but, as I have looked at the governor at his table, from day to day during the hearings of the past three weeks, it has seemed to me, Mr. Chairman, that he has not been happy in his cause; it has seemed to me, from the expression of his face, as I noted it, that something has been troubling him; and, although I listened with

admiration to the very ingenious and eloquent remarks which
he has just delivered, it seemed to me that there was a certain ring wanting in his voice that I have often heard there,
and that his words were not coming from his heart.

Now, gentlemen, all that I can bring to you is a strong,
sincere, and absolute belief in the justice of this petition;
and I wish, at the outset, to examine with you who the parties
are to this contention, and what the contention is; for there
has been so much said and done, both in this chamber and
outside of this chamber, during the past three or four weeks,
that I think perhaps we may have drifted a bit from our
moorings.

WHO FAVOR THE BILL.

Who are the parties, and whom do I represent here? I
represent, first, the Massachusetts Society for the Prevention of Cruelty to Children, — Hon. Frank B. Fay, General
Agent and Secretary, — but, behind that society are almost
all the charitable organizations, or members of them, of this
State, and a very large number of the thinking, charitable
men and women from one end of this Commonwealth to the
other; and, gentlemen, if I should read to you the entire list
of names of persons who favor this bill, I should weary you
in the reading. However, I want to call your attention to
some of them, for there are clergymen, doctors, laymen,
judges of the court, and an ex-governor.

Governor Long has just stated — I forget his exact language
— that no physician or eminent physician has been heard of
upon our side of this case. In reply, let me say that I hold
in my hand at this moment a copy of the leading medical
journal of England, and probably of the world, " The Lancet,"
published at London, January 19, 1895; and I will read you
a few lines from that journal : " The more closely we examine
the practice of child insurance the less there appears to

commend it." "Nor is the position of those who would advocate this system greatly improved when we pass to the
question of ways and means as connected with the event of
an infant's death. Simple in the extreme are all the needful
arrangements for a funeral. Their cost would not overtax
the slender means of almost any family which is maintained
by honest work and thrift, so that even from this point of
view insurance has somewhat the aspect of a superfluity."
" Facts like these" — referring to just such facts as we have
shown you — " tend to sicken the public conscience. They
strongly suggest a necessity for drastic reforms in a system
of somewhat doubtful and limited advantage."

And since Governor Long has intimated that we have no
physicians, or eminent physicians, on our side of this question, let me read to you the names of some of the leading
physicians of Massachusetts who advocate this bill:

Dr. CHARLES F. NICHOLS, *of Boston.*

Dr. JAMES B. BELL, *of Boston.*

Dr. W. F. WESSELHOEFT, *of Boston.*

Dr. W. P. WESSELHOEFT, *of Boston.*

Dr. I. P. HAYWOOD, *of Lynn.*

Dr. GEORGE W. HAYWOOD, *of Lynn.*

Dr. S. MANNING PERKINS, *of Lynn.*

Dr. S. W. CLARK, *City Physician of Lynn.*

Dr. ARTHUR B. CHASE, *City Physician of Lynn.*

Dr. JAMES SHEPHERD, *of Brookline.*

Dr. JULIUS GARST, *of Worcester.*

Dr. AMANDA C. BRAY, *Dispensary Physician of Worcester.*

Dr. S. A. DAVIS.

Dr. H. P. WALCOTT, *Chairman of the State Board of
Health of this Commonwealth.*

Are these gentlemen who would put their names care-
lessly on a petition?

Dr. MALCOLM STORER, another name respected in Boston.

Dr. SAMUEL W. ABBOTT, *Secretary of the State Board of Health.*

Dr. C. C. CHAFFEE, *of Springfield.*

Dr. D. L. OWEN, *of Springfield.*

Dr. C. C. AUSTIN LEACH, — and if that physician, after the testimony which you have listened to at these hearings, does not stand in an enviable place to-day as a lady of undoubted position and veracity, I should like to know a physician in this Commonwealth who does; and for that we have to thank the gentlemen on the other side for giving us an opportunity to let the public know more than they already knew, perhaps, about Dr. Leach, although she has been so favorably known for a *very* long time.

Dr. CHARLES B. THAYER.

Dr. SUSAN D. SHORT.

Dr. JAMES H. PAYNE.

Dr. A. J. BAKER FLINT.

Dr. JOHN P. SUTHERLAND.

Dr. HORACE PACKARD.

Dr. F. P. BATCHELDER.

Dr. I. T. TALBOT, *Dean of Boston University.*

Dr. WINTHROP B. TALBOT.

Dr. A. W. K. NEWTON.

I will pass over a great many names that appear on our petitions, and will mention only a few :

Dr. J. W. WINKLEY.

Dr. GEORGE W. KEITH.

Dr. OLIN M. DRAPER, *of the Massachusetts General Hospital.*

Dr. W. E. PARKER, *of Bowdoin Street.*

Dr. L. M. KIMBALL.

Dr. HENRY J. JORDAN.

Dr. CHARLES L. KINGSBURY.

8

Dr. H. C. CLAPP.

Dr. WILLIAM S. BOARDMAN.

Dr. WALTER WESSELHOEFT, *of Cambridge.*

Dr. HENRY L. DEARING, *of Braintree.*

Dr. SAMUEL C. BRIDGHAM, *of Braintree.*

The governor says that we have no physicians; I shall weary you if I go through my list:

Dr. FRANCIS A. HARRIS, as well known a physician as there is in the State of Massachusetts, and a man who, from his prominent position as Medical Examiner of the county of Suffolk, and because of his intimate acquaintance with crime and want and poverty in the north and west ends of this city, would be the last man to sign a petition in such a matter as this unless it were in accordance with his absolute convictions :

Dr. GEORGE G. SEARS, 17 *Marlboro Street.*

Dr. M. H. BAYNUM, 14 *Hancock Street.*

Dr. A. GASTON ROETH, 105 *Mount Vernon St.*

Dr. EDWARD C. BRIGGS, 125 *Marlboro St.*

Dr. CAROLINE E. HASTINGS, *of School Board.*

Dr. JULIA M. PLUMMER, *Huntington Avenue.*

Dr. C. D. G. MACK, *of Boston.*

Dr. B. F. CAMPBELL, *of Boston.*

Dr. JOSEPH HICKS, 155 *Huntington Avenue.*

Dr. L. D. R. ATKINSON, *of Boston.*

Dr. CHAS. S. ABBOTT, *of Boston.*

Dr. H. F. HAMILTON, 125 *Marlboro Street.*

Dr. C. C. SIMMONS, 114 *Huntington Avenue.*

Dr. ELEANOR F. NEWTON, 528 *Tremont Street.*

Dr. ADALINE B. CHURCH, 102 *Huntington Avenue.*

Dr. NOBLE H. HILL, 9 *Charles Street.*

Dr. JOHN B. BRAINERD, *of Hotel Copley.*

Dr. JOHN H. PAYNE, *of Copley Square.*

Dr. N. H. HOUGHTON, 544 *Columbus Avenue.*

Dr. John F. Harvey, *Tremont Street.*

Dr. Helen G. Mack, *of Boston.*

Dr. J. Heber Smith, *Dartmouth Street, Boston.*

Dr. Geo. M. Palmer, 103 *Mount Vernon Street.*

Those are some of the physicians who are asking you to report this bill.

Now, as to the clergymen,— we have clergymen behind this movement, representing every denomination, eminent clergymen :

Rev. Dr. Alexander McKenzie, *of Cambridge.*

Rev. Minot J. Savage, *of Boston.*

Rev. Philip S. Moxom, *formerly of Boston, now of Springfield.*

Rev. James H. Van Buren, *the Rector of St. Stephen's Church, Lynn.*

Rev. Tillman B. Johnson, *of the First Baptist Church, Lynn.*

Rev. James Reed, and fifty of his church — a prominent man in Boston.

Vicar-General M. F. Byrne.

Rev. Fr. B. F. Killilea.

Rev. Fr. D. J. O'Farrell.

Rev. Fr. Francis X. Dolan.

Rev. Fr. Leo J. Knapp.

Rev. Fr. James Gambera.

Rev. Fr. Joseph Tandolfin.

Rev. Fr. Waldin.

Rev. Fr. Leonard.

All missionaries at the north end of Boston.

Anna M. Knudsen, *Seamen's Missionary, Baptist Bethel.*

Rev. John Welch, *Missionary Baptist Bethel.*

Rev. Walter J. Swaffield, *Missionary Baptist Bethel.*

Emma E. Griffin, *Missionary Baptist Bethel.*

Rev. Elijah How, *Piedmont Church, Worcester.*

ELDREDGE MIX, *Supt. Worcester City Missionary Society.*

A. Z. CONRAD, *Pastor First Church, Worcester.*

JOHN D. PICKLES, *Pastor Trinity M. E. Church.*

B. H. HAYDEN, *Pastor Church of Christ.*

ALMON GUNNISON, *Pastor First Universalist Church.*

T. J. CONATY, *Pastor Sacred Heart Church, Worcester.*

F. B. ALLEN, *Episcopal City Mission.*

Dr. A. A. MINER, *Boston.*

S. H. WINKLEY, *Boston.*

J. J. LANSING, *Park St. Congregational Church.*

HERBERT L. GALE, *Assistant Pastor Congregational Church.*

REGINALD H. HOWE, *Rector Church of our Saviour, Longwood.*

Rev. JOSEPH DURAO, whom you have seen on the witness stand.

Rev. JOHN WELCH.

Rev. BARNARD JOHNSON.

Rev. G. STANLEY HALL, *Dean of Clark University, Worcester.*

Rev. CHARLES L. NOYES, *Somerville.*

Rev. CHRISTOPHER R. ELIOT.

Rev. HERBERT L. GALE.

FRANCES M. GROVES, *Episcopal City Missionary.*

A. L. COVERT, *Episcopal City Missionary.*

JOHN R. HAGUE, *Assistant Pastor Ruggles Street Church.*

W. F. DUSSEAULT, *Malden.*

J. H. REID, *Newburyport.*

EVERETT D. BURR, *Pastor Ruggles Street Church.*

SAMUEL RUSSELL, *Ruggles Street Church.*

A. A. BERLÉ, *Brighton District.*

Rev. Fr. MUNDY, *of Cambridgeport,* whom you saw here, and whom you have heard testify, a man well known in this community,— his parish includes just the class of people among whom a great deal of this insurance is done,— and he told you eloquently and forcibly what his opinion about child insurance was, that he thought it was wrong, as "it was a temptation to neglect life and think more of simply a stylish funeral."

Rev. SAMUEL M. CROTHERS, *of Cambridge.*

Rev. HENRY F. JENKS, *of Canton.*

Rev. ALBERT E. GEORGE, *Rector of St. Matthews Church;* and there are many other clergymen among the petitioners.

Next let me read you the names of some of the persons other than clergymen or physicians — names of sober thinking men and women who are asking for this bill:

Ex-Gov. J. Q. A. BRACKETT.

BARTHOLD SCHLESINGER, *Brookline.*

Hon. STEPHEN SALISBURY, *of Worcester.*

GORHAM D. GILMAN, *Ex-Senator and Hawaiian Consul.*

JOHN READ, *Ex-Senator, Cambridge.*

CHARLES E. DENNISON, *the Dennison Tag Company.*

CHARLES F. DONNELLY, *Boston.*

C. O. L. DILLAWAY, *President of the Mechanics National Bank.*

JAMES W. DUNPHY, *Business Manager of the Advertiser.*

GEORGE E. DANFORTH,
FRED B. WHITING, } *of the Transcript.*
A. H. HAYWARD,

F. H. CUSHMAN, *Editor of the Advertiser.*

T. A. COPELAND, *Editor of the Advertiser.*

B. E. WOOLF, *of the Herald.*

J. W. COVENEY, *Postmaster of Boston.*

WILLIAM T. SHAPLEIGH, *of the Oriental Tea Company.*

WALTER H. ROBERTS, *Law partner of Ex-Governor Brackett.*

MARCUS MORTON, *Director Children's Aid Society.*

JULIUS H. WARD, *Editor of the Herald.*

Frank A. Allen, *Ex-Mayor of Cambridge*, — while this may be a little wearisome to you, gentlemen, yet give me your indulgence, and notice the character of these signatures; they represent the prominent men and women — the thinking men and women of this Commonwealth.

Judge R. E. Harmon, *of Essex County.*

Amos Beckford, *Ex-Representative from Lynn.*

Hon. Stephen Salisbury, *Senator from Worcester.*

Henry A. Marsh, *Mayor of Worcester.*

E. J. Russell, *Probation Officer of Worcester.*

Walter B. Abbott, *of the Young Women's Christian Association of Worcester.*

E. T. Raymond, *Chief Marshal of Worcester.*

Mrs. W. W. Rice, *President of the Temperance Home and Day Nursery Society.*

Mrs. E. L. Connors, *President of the Worcester Women's Club.*

Mrs. Florence M. Stowell, *Superintendent of the Young Women's Christian Association.*

Mr. E. R. Goodwin, *Principal of the "C. H. School."*

Edgar Thompson, *Principal of the Ledge Street School, Worcester.*

Mrs. Willard T. Sears, *well-known in charities, Boston.*

Freeman Brown, *City Almoner.*

Frank P. Kendall, *Treasurer of the Associated Charities of Worcester.*

E. N. Northrop, *Superintendent of the Worcester Boys' Club.*

Mrs. W. B. Lambert, *active worker among poor children, Cambridge.*

P. C. Mendenhall, *President of the Worcester Institute.*

Isabelle E. Stiles, *of the Associated Charities of Worcester.*

Miriam F. Witherspoon, *General Secretary of the Associated Charities of Worcester.*

Geo. H. Worthley, *Brookline.*
Geo. F. Bryce, *Brookline.*
Miss Margaret A. Chapman, *Cambridge.*
Miss Abby L. Alger.
Rev. C. L. D. Younkin, *North End Mission.*
Miss C. V. Drinkwater, *Young Women's Christian Association.*
Miss Sarah G. Buttrick, *Young Women's Christian Association.*
Hon. Geo. H. Carter, *Mayor of Chelsea.*
Thomas Hills, *President South Boston Bank.*
Rev. Dr. Beach, *Cambridge.*
Samuel C. Lawrence, *Children's Aid Society.*
Mrs. E. L. Tuttle and others, *Children's Aid Society.*
Samuel Russell, *Relief Agent Ruggles Street Church.*
Caroline W. Evans,
N. E. Pease,
Fanny Heard,
Caroline T. Hall, } *Associated Charities, Ward 22.*
Francis W. Nichols, *Director Associated Charities.*
Frank M. McLaughlin, *Chief of Melrose.*
Carrie F. Loring, *School Board, East Braintree.*
Irving H. Horne, *Supt. of Schools, Braintree.*
William K. Andem, *Supt. Ruggles St. Bible Society.*
A. H. Mason, *Postmaster, Braintree.*
E. C. Adams, *Principal High School, Newburyport.*
B. S. Wood, *High School, Newburyport.*
M. A. Wood, *High School, Newburyport.*
Amos M. Leonard, *Master Lawrence School.*
George A. Parker, *Probation Officer.*
George P. Eustis, *Asst. Treas. American Rubber Co.*
E. H. Barton, *Treasurer Savings Bank, South Boston.*
M. L. Goodell, *Agent Associated Charities.*
Lizzie N. Collings, *Day Nursery.*
G. E. Freeman, *Boston Children's Aid Society.*
John L. Murray, *Boston.*

John H. Morison, *Boston.*

L. A. Gould, *Superintendent North Bennet Street Industrial School.*

Mrs. T. O. Bemis, *President Hampden County Children's Aid Society.*

Mrs. J. Stuart Kirkham, *Treasurer Hampden County Children's Aid Society.*

Lewis Foster, *Board of Health, Springfield.*

Mrs. Louisa Parsons Hopkins, *Ex-Supervisor of Boston Schools.*

Mrs. H. M. Plunkett, *Pittsfield.*

Willis C. Young, *President of Worcester School Board.*

The governor has cited the name of a clergyman of the Phillips Church as opposed to the petition, but it appeared in evidence that this clergyman was at one time connected with the insurance business, and here are fifteen or twenty names of prominent members of his parish who are *in favor* of the bill. Then we find the name of

Jabez B. Cole, *of Boston, Undertaker;* and so on; I will not read any more.

And now right here, since some mention has been made—either by the governor or by his witnesses — that we are only a few philanthropic people in *Boston,* let me call your attention to the cities and towns from which petitions have come : —

Cambridge, Boston, Somerville, Winchester, Allston, Malden, Centreville, Lynn, Worcester, Orleans, Melrose, Amesbury, Brookline, Springfield, Medford, Chelsea, Salem, Beachmont, West Roxbury, Waverley, Dorchester, Everett, Atlantic, Quincy, Forest Hills, Jamaica Plain, Lowell, Hyde Park, Charlestown, Waltham, Newton, Wellesley, Canton, Newburyport, Braintree, East Braintree, South Braintree, Portsmouth —

I will not read any more, although there are still many other places represented in this movement.

OPPONENTS OF THE BILL.

Arrayed against the petitioners who have and who can have no interest in this matter, except for the *welfare of little children*, are the three great corporations, The Metropolitan, the John Hancock, and the Prudential, with their millions of capital, their great buildings, their enormous salaries, their thousands of agents, with every self interest at stake, fighting for the *welfare* of *the corporations!*

And the argument has been advanced that this bill should not be passed because the result would be that a great many men would be thrown out of employment. But if the system is *wrong*, that argument should have no weight. It might as well be claimed, for the same reason, that the Louisiana Lottery and the endowment orders should not have been driven *out of this State.*

That, gentlemen, shows you how we stand before you. Now, the governor comes here with petitions representing 50,000 names, and I do not doubt that before this matter is discussed in the House, — and I am hopeful that it will be discussed there, — I do not doubt that there will be 75,000 names, because the insurance companies are powerful, and their agents number 5,000 men in this State; therefore, if each one of these men signs a petition, and asks his wife and a few of his friends to sign their names too, you will see how easily the number of names on the petitions must roll up. So let the companies' agents gather in their 75,000 names of persons, but I ask your careful attention to the very exceptional character of the 2,000 names of earnest thinking men and women throughout this Commonwealth who advocate the passage of this bill.

CHILD MURDER NOT CLAIMED.

What is the contention here? Mr. Chairman, I never yet in my life have met such a remarkable party of gentlemen — gentlemen who seem to find it so difficult to understand the English language! Whenever I put a question to Vice-President Fiske which he did not wish to answer, he would at once reply, "I can't understand you; I really can't understand what you mean; if anybody can see what your meaning is, I should like to know it." I stated in my opening remarks the position of the petitioners,— that we did not come here asking you to legislate because child *murder* was going on in this State. You will remember it, gentlemen, I am sure, for it is plainly stated in the stenographic report. That is what I stated, and the other side interrupted me and contended that I *did* claim *murder*, and this has been the cry of the numerous attorneys for the insurance companies throughout the hearings. Indeed, it would seem as if they had prepared their defence upon that ground, and could not and dared not meet our true position, — that helpless *living* children were suffering and neglected through the evils of child insurance. That was my contention, and the claim of child murder was disavowed by me again and again throughout the hearings.

I stated our position clearly and plainly,— that we came here as charitable workers among the poor, looking after the interests of the children, and that we were trying to protect *living* children, desiring to prevent their being subjected to starvation and neglect while they *were alive*, but I could not succeed in making these gentlemen understand it, and apparently even the governor does not, or *will not* understand it to-day!

The vice-president of the largest of these companies, the Metropolitan, of New York, the company which has $22,000,000 assets, the greater part of which amount has come, as I will show you in a few moments, from monthly payments by the poor policy holders of $1,000,000 a month in five and ten cent pieces, and from the really frightful amount of money lost by the poor and gained by the companies in lapsed policies — the vice-president of that company, in reply to me, when I said, "You do not understand me, — I am not claiming that these children are *murdered*," answered, "Well, that is what you *did* claim." "Excuse me," I replied, "I have not claimed it, and here is the evidence to show it, in type," as I have been obliged to prove my statements to the attorneys for the insurance companies a number of times during these hearings from the stenographic report, — and I think, if I may be permitted to say so, whenever I have appealed to that report, the report has verified my statements. When I told the vice-president of the New York Company that I did not claim that there was child *murder*, he replied, "But you have claimed it, and have withdrawn from that position." "Excuse me," I answered, "I have not withdrawn from it, because I could not have withdrawn from a position which I had never taken." "Well, then," said he, in reply, "if you did not claim it, you *meant* to claim it"; and that is the vice-president's logic!

Gentlemen of the committee, why does Vice-President Fiske and why do the many attorneys of the insurance companies insist on claiming that the issue here is child *murder?* I will tell you why, — they understand my English only too well, but they *cannot* and they *dare not* meet our position, — that helpless *living* children are suffering and neglected through the evils of child insurance, and so they raise a false issue, and with sounding words assail that issue, thinking that they may deceive you and lead your minds away from the true issue, when in reality they have in no way met our allegations.

But, gentlemen, they *will not deceive you!*

ORIGIN OF THE MOVEMENT.

Before considering the witnesses and the nature of the testimony on one side and the other, I wish now to refer to a matter that has been brought forward by Mr. Fiske. It was claimed by the insurance companies that the petitioners began this movement by drawing the bill, and that then they hastened about to get evidence to support it. I need not spend much time on that claim, for you have heard the evidence; you have heard the testimony of Mrs. Atwood that eight years ago this matter was first considered by her, and that last summer, almost a year ago, a case in court, which my friend, Mr. Charles E. Haywood, tried, — a very painful case, — suggested the matter more directly to her attention, and to the attention of the Society for the Prevention of Cruelty to Children; and that in December last, that honest-faced ex-policeman and now officer of the society, Mr. Monsier D. Mann, — and a more honest face has never appeared before a committee in this State House, — brought the matter up again, and it went into the hands of a committee in January, and the result was the petition which has been presented for the passage of this bill offered by the Massachusetts Society for the Prevention of Cruelty to Children. Why should Mr. Fiske make so absurd a statement as that, — that we first thought of this bill only a few weeks ago, and that since then we have been looking up evidence to support it !

THE MASSACHUSETTS SOCIETY IN 1891.

One other point let me dispose of now. A good deal of comment has been made because the report of the Society for the Prevention of Cruelty to Children in 1891, did not seem to take the same position that the Society is taking now ; and Governor Long called the attention of this committee to this report, in which was this clause : " We find in English reports that parents are charged with insuring the lives of their children, in order, by neglect, if by no worse crime, *to destroy* the child to secure the insurance. We have taken pains to inquire into this practice here, but have found no evidence of *such intent*, although many insure their children's lives." That is to say, Mr. Fay in 1891, for the Society for the Prevention of Cruelty to Children, made some investigation as to whether *murder* was going on here in Boston, intentional *murder*, as was said to be the case in England, and not finding that state of things existing, he passed the matter by.

ACTION OF OTHER SOCIETIES.

Since that time the matter of child insurance has received increased attention in this country, and in 1892 the American Humane Society for the Prevention of Cruelty to Animals and Children, comprising the charitable associations of the country, reported as follows : " Whereas, it has been brought to the notice of this Association, of the existence of child insurance in many of our States, therefore be it

Resolved, That each Society for the Prevention of Cruelty to Children be requested to make this a special feature of investigation, and report at our next meeting." People were

beginning to look into the matter in 1892. That was the *next
year* after Mr. Fay had written his report. And the *following year*, in *1893*, another step was taken, and this resolution was passed at Chicago by this same national association
with regard to child insurance : —

"*Resolved*, That it is the sense of this body that the practice of insuring the lives of children under ten years of age,
under any pretext, is *against public policy*, and is so great
an incentive to crime that it becomes the duty of all who
are interested in humane work to use their best endeavors to
procure, at the earliest possible moment, the passage of such
laws as shall effectually prohibit a practice so dangerous in
any part of the United States ; and the secretary of this
national organization is hereby instructed to prepare printed
matter in some form, setting forth these facts, and distribute
the same among the various local organizations under his
jurisdiction, and ask their co-operation in procuring, at the
next session of the Legislature in the various States (not
already having such provision), such laws as shall make it a
criminal offence for any person, persons, or corporation to
insure the life of a child, or in any manner offer a reward
upon the death of a child."

That resolution, Mr. Chairman and gentlemen, passed by
this national organization at Chicago in 1893, the American
Humane Association, that child insurance was a thing that must
be examined and looked into by all the societies connected
with that association throughout the country, is entitled
to very great weight. And please consider that resolution
in connection with the facts that I will now give you, as to
how some of these companies have been galloping on in this
matter of child insurance. Why, gentlemen, unless you
look at the figures, you can have no idea of the rate at
which they are increasing in business. There are now
100,000 children in Massachusetts under ten years of age

who are insured, and if these companies continue to swell their business at the present rate, in a few years every child in the State under ten years of age will be insured.

To show how rapidly the companies are growing in wealth, let me state that, in 1879, the assets of the Metropolitan Company were $2,034,042.78, — in 1889, $8,597,468.77, — in 1894, $22,326,622.16, increasing from two millions to twenty-two millions in fifteen years, and its income increased in the same proportion, — in 1879, $567,598.51, — in 1889, $8,725,196.47, — and in 1894, $18,208,742.75.

I tell you, Mr. Chairman and gentlemen of this committee, it is getting to be a pretty serious matter, when one company is able to so increase in wealth in fifteen years. And still another company, the Prudential, has now, within a few months, come into the State, attracted by this splendid field. So you see that the condition of affairs is very different in 1895 from that in 1891, and Mr. Fay *now* finds that the little children of this State need protection from these grasping corporations, and so he comes to you in their behalf for aid.

I submit that their comment upon Mr. Fay's position as to his report in 1891 is fully answered.

EVIDENCE OF THE INSURANCE COMPANIES

Having shown you who are the parties and what the contention is, I will now call your attention to the witnesses and the evidence on either side. I do not propose, however, in the brief time that has been allowed for argument, to attempt any elaborate discussion of the evidence which has been introduced. You have looked upon the witnesses, you have listened to their statements, and I am content that you should now decide whether the insurance companies have controlled or even met our allegations, and whether we have not abundantly proved the existence in our midst of a system that calls for immediate action by the Legislature.

Governor Long in his argument said, " We brought swarms of witnesses here from Lowell, from Lawrence, from Boston, from Worcester, from Fall River — everywhere. What an array we have given you ! "

As a matter of fact, the Governor introduced a large number of letters, a great many of them being very short and containing merely negative statements, and brought before you twenty-one witnesses who testified.

Of these, one was the president of the Prudential, one the vice-president of the Metropolitan, and one the medical examiner of the John Hancock, all three, of course, being intensely interested witnesses. Of the remainder of the twenty-one, seven, including three clergymen, were or *had been insurance agents*, or in some way connected with these very insurance companies, and one represented a newspaper which makes a specialty of insurance matters. Thus out of those twenty-one witnesses, eleven, or more than one half, were *interested* witnesses, and of the remaining ten, several testified that they knew but little about child insurance and the very poor districts.

The Governor is a very fluent speaker, but I am afraid he was drawing heavily upon his imagination when he spoke of his " swarms of witnesses," and when you scrutinize the witnesses which he actually brought, you find that they are reduced practically to the three persons already referred to, Mr. John F. Dryden, of the Prudential, Mr. Haley Fiske, of the Metropolitan, and Dr. Frank Wells, of the John Hancock, and the evidence of each of these gentlemen is mainly addressed to the broad subject of industrial insurance and its benefits, and to proving that child insurance does not cause *child murder*.

We have shown you that we have not claimed and do not claim that child insurance causes child murder, and the claim that we are attacking industrial insurance is too absurd to need a reply.

The companies have also introduced a large number of letters, a great many of them very short letters and containing merely negative statements. Why do not the people come here? In the presentation of my side of the case I have brought you face to face with nearly all the witnesses who have had opinions to express in behalf of the bill. But many of the witnesses of the remonstrants testify by letters. Who the people are who write, under what circumstances the letters are written, and whether or not the writers know about poverty and child insurance, — that is all unknown to us, and it is all unknown to you. What weight can such letters have?

Take for instance the Sister Pamela letter that Governor Long relies upon so strongly. What is this Child's Hospital in New York; is it large or is it small? Who is sister Pamela. What does she really know about the needs of the poorer classes? And after all, her testimony is *negative*, for she said, "I have *never known* such a child to be neglected or its death hastened." She too is thinking of child *murder*, and there may have been countless cases of neglect even if she has never known about them!

Governor Long says that "frantic efforts" have been made by us to get her to change this letter. That statement is absolutely unfounded, — *we have never made the slightest attempt to do so*, for we do not think the letter is of importance.

Is that letter to be considered one moment in comparison with the clear, *positive* testimony of such a woman as Mrs. Atwood?

And with regard to Sister Pamela's letter as she speaks of the mother's love for her children, let me quote a few lines from a recent article in a Boston newspaper from the pen of a trustee of the Avon Home, Cambridge:

"How can the true mother, though poor, grieving just as tenderly and truly as if she were rich, take any comfort in the sight of more elaborate funeral surroundings than she otherwise could have had, if the first thought that comes to her in her agony, — for the loss of a child is agony, nothing more nor less, — is, 'Oh, if I had only spent the money that has brought me these things for the funeral, all through my child's little life, to build it up and strengthen it, perhaps it would not have been lying here now.' It seems to me that the showy hearse and white casket would increase the agony tenfold to any mother who has the true mother love in her heart; and are we not trying to implant the true and holy mother love in all classes, rich as well as poor, instead of a mistaken love, that can be comforted as Sister Pamela says, by a funeral! It seems to me she cannot understand what true mother love is with its holy, self-sacrificing devotion."

And as bearing upon Sister Pamela's letter, I will also read the following letter, lately written from the convent of Our Lady of Good Counsel, an association for befriending children and young girls, at White Plains, N. Y.

"We take this occasion to speak of a custom among the poor, at present, which needs looking after. If a child is delicate they get its life insured, and then they put it in an institution. Nine out of ten of the cases sent here are insured to the extent of sixty or eighty dollars. The child dies; they are satisfied; they do not come until they are sure the child is buried; then some official calls for proof that the child has died, and the parents collect the money. In the meantime, the general expenses to us have been from ten to fifteen dollars. We have for some time desired to lay this matter before your consideration, not from purely personal motives, but because it is an imposition on the public.

Very truly,

SISTER MARY ZITA,
In charge of the House of Nazareth.

MARASMUS.

A single word as to marasmus. Mrs. Atwood's position was, that there had been many cases of marasmus in 1893. Dr. Wells, attempting to contradict her, stated that according to certain statistics there had been only one death from marasmus in 1893, when Mrs. Atwood at once produced a *verified* list from the city registrar's office in Boston, showing that there had been about three hundred deaths from marasmus between July 1 and November 16, 1893. Dr. Wells was mistaken in this matter, as he has been in other matters during this hearing.

THE TYPOGRAPHICAL UNION RESOLUTION.

There is one other piece of evidence that I wish to refer to, and that is the Typographical Union Resolution. I do not care to dwell upon this matter at any length, but I think the attempt to offer this piece of evidence was as extraordinary a proceeding as I ever witnessed at a hearing or in a court room. The resolution was presented to this committee and placed upon your table with the intimation that it was the act of a body of sixteen or eighteen hundred men who in calm deliberation had passed it, when the fact was, as I discovered upon examining it, that the preamble of the resolution had been cut out by the counsel for the insurance companies, although it was vital to the resolution, which, without the preamble, could never have been passed, — and further, that the preamble was wholly false and misleading. Facts were subsequently brought out at the hearing which tended to show that the resolution had been drafted and introduced by an agent of one of the industrial insurance companies, and that instead of sixteen or eighteen hundred men there were only two or three hundred present at the meeting — which was an ordinary monthly meeting and *not* called for this particular purpose!

(See Vol. 13, pp. 18, 19, 20.)

Such a proceeding on the part of the counsel for the insurance companies cannot be justified. It clearly proves that the case of the remonstrants is a desperate and a bad one, when such measures are resorted to.

EVIDENCE OF THE PETITIONERS.

On the other hand, the evidence of the petitioners comes from wholly disinterested persons, nearly all of whom have appeared before you in person and spoken from personal knowledge.

The counsel upon the other side have fiercely attacked the dozen or more cases testified to by Mrs. Atwood, but I submit, gentlemen, with entire confidence, that they have not thrown a doubt upon a single case; on the contrary, I claim that these cases are stronger to-day than when they were first put in evidence. You will remember how convincing was the testimony of those three ladies, Mrs. Atwood, Dr. Leach and Miss Frenyear, who spoke to you from an intimate personal knowledge of the subject under investigation, and after a long experience in charity work, and you will remember, too, how the counsel for the companies attacked each one of those estimable women.

They attacked Dr. Leach, I am sorry to say, with insult. They attacked Miss Frenyear with compliment, and tried to elbow her out of this committee room with sarcasm and sarcastic praise; and they attacked Mrs. Atwood by attempting to prove that her statements were not true. I say,

attempting to prove; for how did those attempts succeed?
I submit that the evidence was clear and strong in her favor,
and that Mrs. Atwood's cases were every one of them sus-
tained. Dr. Leach submitted one hundred cases and stated
that she could give you one thousand. Her statements also
are uncontradicted. Mrs. Atwood, when she left the stand,
said that, having told you in detail of those twelve or more
cases, she would offer no more then, fearing that she might
weary you; she stated, however, that if you should wish to
hear more similar cases, she could easily bring you fifty or
one hundred. Miss Frenyear also offered many cases and
they are unchallenged. So, against the officers of these
wealthy corporations looking for their own gain, stand those
three noble women whose life work consists in doing good,
— in caring for the sick, in helping the unfortunate, — noble
women, who, in the spirit of Him who said, "Suffer little
children to come unto me," are devoting their lives to works
of charity and kindness and benevolence. God bless them,
say I.

And it did not very well become the counsel upon the
other side to throw the slurs and the insults and the insinu-
ations which they did upon one, at least, of these good women.
But she has come out only brighter from the ordeal.

I submit, gentlemen, that the evidence of each one of
these disinterested women is unimpeached and unimpeach-
able to-day. And when you recollect that their evidence is
supported by the mass of testimony from those earnest,
impressive witnesses, Hon. Frank B. Fay, Rev. Albert E.
George, Edward Atkinson, R. H. Dana, Mr. Mann, Mrs.
Alice L. Taylor, Mr. Roberts, Dr. J. Heber Smith, Dr.
Charles Mack, Rev. Father Mundy, Rev. D. N. Beach, Dr.
Helen G. Mack, W. W. Towle, Rev. E. D. Burr, Rev.
Samuel Russell, Rev. A. A. Berlé, Joseph Bennett, Dr. A.
A. Miner, John H. Morison, Rev. C. L. Noyes, Rev. Joseph

F. Durao, and also by the numerous very strong letters from Rev. M. J. Savage, Rev. Philip S. Moxom, Dr. Alexander McKenzie, C. F. Donnelly, Esq., and many others, — when you recollect this, you cannot fail to be convinced of the justice of our cause and that this bill ought to become a law.

LETTERS.

CHURCH OF THE UNITY STUDY, PEMBROKE STREET.

BOSTON, March 29, 1895.

CHAS. READ, Esq.,

Dear Sir, — I write a word only to tell you how much I sympathize with you in your fight for the children ! Until fathers and mothers cease to be brutal and drunken, it is not safe to put them in the way of such a temptation as this child insurance. I think you have the best heads and hearts of Boston with you.

Most sincerely,

(Signed) M. J. SAVAGE.

MARCH 26, 1895.

MR. READ,

Dear Sir, — In company with many others I have been shocked and sickened by the recent revelations in connection with " child insurance." May I express through you my conviction that such things should be rendered impossible in the future by prompt and adequate legislation. I can think of no sufficient justification for the existence of companies that engage in such a business as has been so tragically brought before the public mind in connection with child life and death. Sincerely yours,

(Signed) PHILIP S. MOXOM.

THE FIRST CHURCH IN CAMBRIDGE.

CAMBRIDGE, MASS., March 16, 1895.

My Dear Mr. Read, — I want to add my word to the words of the many whom you represent in the effort to break up the cruel and dangerous business of child insurance. I had no idea of the extent to which this traffic in the lives of children is carried until the matter was brought into the light by the evidence laid before the legislative committee, and published in the papers. I do not see what can be said in its defence. It is beyond question that this system of staking money upon the life of a child a year or two old is full of peril. The class of persons to which the solicitation to insure the lives of their children is persistently presented should be protected and not imperilled. They are poor, and in many cases dependent upon charity. To make the death of their children a pecuniary advantage is the most merciless manner of temptation of which I have any knowledge. It is not necessary to prove murder, or even to prove absolute neglect. The danger is evident. It surprises me that men are willing to throw even the possibility of such crime in the way of those who would not be unlikely to yield to it. I cannot go before the committee with my appeal. I wish that through you I might urge them to put an immediate and certain end to this flagrant evil.

Yours very truly,

(Signed) ALEXANDER McKENZIE.

35 COURT STREET, BOSTON, March 18, 1895.

CHARLES C. READ, Esq.,

Dear Sir, — I regret that I cannot attend the legislative hearing on the bill against child insurance, but will give, as you request, my views on the subject.

It seems to me, the business of insuring the lives of children should not be countenanced by law, and that the sooner the Legislature will intervene to prevent it, the better for the community.

. . . .

To my mind the law should not only prevent insurance on the lives of children, but upon the life of any minor, unless the insured appeared to be dependent chiefly upon him for support.

. . . .

The whole of the present contention narrows itself down to the question, Can any reflecting citizen of Massachusetts justify himself in assisting in maintaining the unnatural practice of bargaining and speculating on the lives of the very young, the helpless and the unprotected? It is certainly not too much to claim that there should be no bargaining or trafficking in our Commonwealth under her auspices, in infant life, which has been held sacred under the higher law of nature in all times, and which, even under the artificial conditions of our high civilization to-day, is yet generally guarded and cherished.

Yours truly,

(Signed) CHAS. F. DONNELLY.

GOVERNOR LONG'S MISLEADING COMMENTS ON CASES.

CASE 1.

Governor Long comments on Mrs. Atwood's case No. 1, and asks what has this "to do with the matter of child insurance"!

Mrs. Atwood testified that she had known this family for eight years, and that the condition of the house was filthy in the extreme; that the children were terribly neglected, that she had helped them a great many times, and that the drunken husband earned sometimes $2.50 a week — once $4.00 — and some weeks nothing, and that they paid forty cents a week on insurance of the six children and the father; that she saw the insurance books and that they were insured in the John Hancock.

To contradict this evidence of Mrs. Atwood, Governor Long produced Dr. Brechin, who was a paid examiner of the John Hancock, who testified that he never had visited the family before, but was sent there after Mrs. Atwood had testified, to examine the children; that he stayed in the house only "a half or three quarters of an hour," in which time he had to run over them all (all six children) and ask the various questions on the blanks.

He verified largely Mrs. Atwood's testimony, and contradicted himself, stating (see Vol. 12, p. 79) that he had looked for sore eyes because it *was mentioned in the testimony*, and afterwards (see Vol. 12, p. 81), that he did not know till afterwards what Mrs. Atwood had testified. And he admitted that the place might have been in a very different condition then from its condition when Mrs. Atwood saw it; he also stated that about $35 a week was earned by the father and boys.

Can Mrs. Atwood's testimony be discredited at all by this hasty examination of a *paid insurance man*, sent to contradict her, who only stayed a half or three quarters of an hour? Mrs. Atwood told you she had personally known this family for eight years, and at various times had assisted it, — this doctor, in the company's employ, looks at them for half an hour, and tells you they earn five dollars a day, and are a lovely family! Which will you believe?

But it is admitted *that the John Hancock had insured them!*

Still Governor Long asks "what has this case to do with child insurance" ! !

CASE 2.

Governor Long says that if anything was wrong, it was not due to insurance. That case was cited to show you that the insurance agents do insure children in the very poorest families, — where the parents cannot afford to pay the premiums, — and the immediate result is neglect of the children.

This woman was a drinking woman and could not support her child, but the insurance agent induced her to pay twenty-five cents in advance for insurance.

THE CRESSEY CASE.

Governor Long is amazed that I spent so much time on this case. Doubtless he would have preferred that I should not have spent any time on it! The family was one of the worst, most filthy, most wretched, most drunken in Boston, — two little children died from neglect, — a family wretchedly poor, and yet the insurance agents went there and the only child that was old enough was insured!

Governor Long says that it is "unfair, unjust and malignant" to attack the companies with a case like that! He also says that Mrs. Atwood left the impression that the two children who died were insured, and that that created a false impression on the public!

Allow me to call Governor Long's attention to Volume 2, page 25 of the evidence, where, on the second day of this hearing, when Mrs. Atwood first told of this case, we read, "(By the CHAIRMAN.) Did I understand you to state that the two who died were insured? *A.* They were *not insured.*"

Governor Long should read the evidence correctly before he charges us with being "unfair, unjust and malignant."

And the governor asks, What has that case to do with child insurance? I answer, It has very much to do with it, for it shows how the agents swarm through the slums.

CASE 3.

Governor Long has referred to Mrs. Atwood's case of wretched drunkenness, — father a maniac when in liquor, etc. This is Mrs. Atwood's case No. 3. Father, mother and six children, *all insured except the mother;* father is a drunkard; for five months the family absolutely destitute. Mrs. Atwood speaks from her own personal knowledge; one day only a small crust and not a mouthful of food for mother and six children; Mrs. Atwood had helped to pay their rent; everything mortgaged; greatest want and poverty; yet *all insured* except the mother.

The only defence offered is a short letter *written on an insurance blank purporting* to have been written by the woman. An insurance agent called on her six days after Mrs. Atwood's testimony, entered the house a stranger to the woman, described the woman as "a pleasant-faced looking lady, with a family of rosy-cheeked children about her." And the agent *says* she wrote this letter saying that she never had received assistance!

Governor Long is indeed fighting a desperate battle when
he places such evidence as that against the statement of Mrs.
Atwood that the family was wretchedly, pitifully destitute,
and that she had constantly assisted them.

And in this wretched family the father and six children
were insured!

And Governor Long says: "Indeed, in such a family,
insurance would seem to be a good thing"!

THE FINN CASE.

With regard to the wretched Finn Case, Governor Long
states that the children were not insured — but Dr. Wells
admitted that *a policy had been taken out on one of them,*
although he stated that it had been given up.

(See Vol. 12, p. 27.)

Officer Mann's account of the condition of the house was
sickening; and in this case, the insurance companies produced a certificate of one Dr. Conn to support their case,
and the certificate of Dr. Conn was conclusively proved to
have been *false.* Dr. Conn was requested by both sides to
come here, but of course he did not dare to do so; for the
evidence was clear and strong that Dr. Conn had stated to
several persons that the children died of starvation, as Mrs.
Atwood had testified.

This case is of importance, as it shows the methods of the
insurance companies, and into what kind of families the
agents go. Governor Long says, What does it amount to —
as children were not insured? but *insurance had been taken*
out and the agents had been there. If there was no insurance at the time of death, yet the case is very important as
showing that the agents try to place insurance in such poor,
wretched families.

CASE OF YOUNG WOMAN GONE TO WESTERN ISLANDS.

Mrs. Atwood stated that this child was insured and taken to the West End Nursery in a very neglected condition. Child was illegitimate, certificate of death refused by the doctor.

Mrs. Atwood's statements are corroborated by Missionary Rev. J. F. Durao and by two written statements, also by certificate from the West End Nursery.

To rebut these statements, Governor Long offers the affidavit of three Portuguese women, stating merely that they did not *know* of child being neglected, and the affidavits were all written in English — interpreted to the women — two of whom were so illiterate *that they signed by mark.*

And Governor Long says that "Mrs. Atwood said the doctor refused to give certificate, and yet we produced the certificate signed by the doctor, Dr. John Dane"!

This statement of Governor Long, if unexplained, would apparently throw discredit upon Mrs. Atwood's statement; it would have been fairer if Governor Long had said that Mrs. Atwood referred to *Dr. Pease of* 15 *Charles Street,* who attended the child, and *not* to Dr. Dane. Who is Dr. Dane, and what evidence is there that *he* ever attended the child?

CASE OF TWO CHILDREN INSURED IN THE METRO-POLITAN, WHO DIED IN SUMMER OF 1894.

Mrs. Atwood testified that the mother of the children said that she often went without food herself, and compelled the children to go without food, to pay the insurance money.

Mrs. Atwood's testimony is corroborated by the original records from the Society for the Prevention of Cruelty to

Children, also by the Rev. 'J. F. Durao, Missionary, who testified that the mother made similar statements to him.

To meet this strong evidence from Mrs. Atwood, Rev. Mr. Durao, and the records, Governor Long brings the Vice-Consul (not the Consul, as Governor Long said), who stated that he did not know the woman and had never called on her before, but after Mrs. Atwood's evidence he went to see her, *with one of the insurance agents*, stayed *ten or fifteen minutes*, and there the woman denied that she or the children went without food to pay the insurance premiums! Would she have said to these strangers anything different? And will such evidence as that disprove Mrs. Atwood's and Mr. Durao's testimony, supported by the record book?

And yet Governor Long says, "How can you account for such gross misrepresentation," etc.?

Does he mean the misrepresentation of Mrs. Atwood or the absurd misrepresentation of his own witness, the Vice-Consul?

CASE OF MOTHER INSURED FOR ONE YEAR IN THE METROPOLITAN FOR $125. — COMPANY PAID BUT $29.

The statement of Governor Long with regard to this case is very misleading.

He states that Mrs. Atwood testified that this mother was insured for $125, but that the company paid only $29, while, says Governor Long, we showed you by the affidavit of Daniel Collins that the *full amount* according to the terms of the policy was received, — just as if Mrs. Atwood was wrong in stating that the company paid only $29, and that the company had really paid *$125* instead of *$29*.

But *$29 was the full amount according to the terms* of this policy, dying when she did.

(See Vol. 12, p. 31, evidence).

And, therefore, Mrs. Atwood's testimony was exactly correct.

If Governor Long's cause is good, why does he constantly make these misleading statements?

Governor Long further states that the three children *are provided for* and never have been neglected.

But the affidavit shows that one little girl has left home and gone to live with a friend, and a second little girl is living with a cousin, — therefore they evidently did need help, as Mrs. Atwood testified.

SHAWMUT AVENUE CASE.

Governor Long speaks of this case as if we had cited it on the ground that criminal proceedings might be justified. We did nothing of the sort. Again Governor Long states that Dr. J. Heber Smith was rather in favor of child insurance ; but that is not so.

Dr. Smith said "my opinion is unfavorable to the existing of (child) insurance, with the present want of limitation."

(See Vol. 4, p. 11.)

Again Governor Long is mistaken in saying that Dr. Helen Mack stated there was snow on the ground October 15. She did not so state She said "I *think* there was snow —I won't state — I don't know."

(Vol. 5, p. 31.)

Again Governor Long is in error as to Dr. Chas. Mack. He was not there during the days when Dr. Helen Mack was there, but *subsequently*, so he does not contradict her as to the fire.

Inspector Dugan visited the place *five months* after Dr. Helen Mack, and he derived his information from Mrs. Tyler, who, he admits, was a woman of less than average intelligence. The statements of Dr. Helen G. Mack and Dr. J. Heber Smith are to be believed.

And we have proved all that we claimed to prove, — that insurance agents go to such places, insuring children for the benefit of persons not parents, and that this child was insured by the keeper of this house.

(Vol. 5, p. 15 — Vol. 11, p. 50.)

THE ROACH CASE.

This was not one of Mrs. Atwood's cases, and is unimportant.

Governor Long says, "That is the way these cases petered out."

On the contrary, I submit that every one of Mrs. Atwood's cases have been proved conclusively and beyond a doubt, in spite of the adroit methods employed by the counsel on the other side to overcome then, and his misleading statements made with regard to them.

I am sorry to see these misleading statements coming from Governor Long, but I more regret the use by him of the words with which he closed his argument. He asked the committee to reject the bill, "not merely as counsel," but "as an officer in the Society for the Prevention of Cruelty to Children"! The Board of Directors of this society, on February 6, 1895, by a formal vote at a duly called meeting, unanimously voted to favor with counsel the passage of this bill before the Legislature. Governor Long was, and is, a vice-president of this society. Nevertheless, without first severing his connections with the society, he accepted a retainer from a rich corporation and *led* a contest *against* the society. And more than that: he asked the committee on insurance to reject the bill, not merely because he was counsel for the insurance companies, but *for the very reason that he was an officer in the charitable society against which he was leading the attack, which society had duly voted to favor the bill!*

This personal argument was an extraordinary one, to say the least, and that Governor Long should have felt obliged to use it argues that his cause is indeed desperate.

THE INSURANCE AGENTS AND THEIR METHODS.

Much has been said about the insurance agents, and I wish to say a few words to you, gentlemen, about these agents and their methods in obtaining child insurance. You will remember that there are about 5,000 of these agents in Massachusetts, — persistent, sharp, shrewd men. You will remember also, that in my opening remarks I produced before you a Metropolitan instruction book for agents, and as it is so many weeks since this case was opened, I will read to you again some of the instructions contained in this book.

"The agent will make it his first duty to master the con_ tents of this book, and then follow them to the letter. He must be an energetic, persevering canvasser," or solicitor, "visiting *every family* in his district, and going systematically from *house to house, floor to floor*, and *room to room*, and *repeating* his visits until every person whom it is possible to insure has been *secured*." Notice the word *secured*! "Begin Monday morning bright and early, put in long days, and keep it up until every member has been visited — give every minute possible to canvassing for new business — better a little field well tilled than a big one half worked — push your work quietly; the *still hunt* is the one that tells. *Stick to your field — don't skim over it*, but dig deeply — keep cool — *use tact.*"

You will remember also how the president of the Metropolitan interrupted me with the remark, "But that book which you are reading from is seven years old!" He intended to imply that they did not so instruct their agents now. But to-day I hold in my hand a book of instructions, dated *1893*, the latest that has been published; and this book contains the same instructions to agents which the other contained! So the president of the Metropolitan, when he made that remark, was either misinformed, or was attempting to mislead this committee!

The evidence has proved to you that these agents swarm through the poorest districts of the cities and through the slums.

You have heard the testimony, — how the pay of the agents depends largely on their own work; how the more they hustle, the more they can make; how, in one company, the agent receives fifteen times the first week's premiums on the net increase of new insurance written by him, and fifteen per cent of all subsequent premiums collected by him; and, in addition, receives at the end of three months, as a quarterly compensation, five times the amount of net increase that he has been able to hold during the three months; and how, at the end of one year, the company will pay the agent, if he still continues their agent, and has not been turned out, a present of $100; at the end of two years, $200; and at the end of three years, $300; how meetings are held every week; how prizes are offered of gold dollars and five-dollar gold pieces and ten-dollar gold pieces and gold watches for the best work; how the names of the most successful canvassers, the men who get the greatest applications in a week or a month, are posted up on the walls at their meetings; how one man, who gets the greatest number of applications in a week or a month, receives a prize of a free ticket to New York, and another, a suit of clothes; and how they have a system of rivalry with flags.

The insurance companies offer these prizes, and have

these weekly meetings of the agents to work upon their feelings, so that they will go out with the greatest ardor and enthusiasm among the poor people. And they do another thing. At these weekly meetings, when all is excitement, the superintendents distribute songs to the men to sing ; and perhaps you would like to hear a few words from one of them, for I have a copy here. These gentlemen are not satisfied merely to *talk* to their agents. That is not sufficient. They want to work upon their feelings, to excite them to the highest pitch of enthusiasm, and they are very skilful in accomplishing this. This is a song from the Metropolitan Company, and the vice-president of that company, if he arranged the song, did it with very great skill, because the music is,— I am not going to sing it, gentlemen, — (*Laughter.*) I am not going to sing it, but I will tell you what the music is, — it is the air that the Union soldiers sang when they were making that magnificent march across Georgia, from Atlanta to the sea.

Let me read a verse to you. Imagine these men gathered at their weekly meeting ; the enthusiasm is running high with the flags and the gold prizes, and by and by in comes the superintendent and cries out, " Now, boys, let's have a song," and the agents all begin to sing. Let me read one verse to you :

We 're the Metropolitan Legion,
We 're the victors in the fray,
We 've waged the battle earnestly,
At last have won the day;
We are here to wear the laurel wreath
The company's bestowed,
In this great Metropolitan City.

Hurrah ! Hurrah ! we 'll sound the jubilee!
Hurrah! Hurrah! we 've won the victory!
We 've laid aside our toils and care, from duty we are free
While enjoying the reward bestowed upon us.

When our leader ordered " Forward, boys!"
We rallied to his call;
Responses prompt and loyal,
No doubts nor fears appall;
We saw Victory in the distance,
And a Furlough in the fall,
In this great Metropolitan City.

Hurrah! Hurrah! etc.

We never wavered in the fight,
Pressed forward night and day,
Kept at it " *everlastingly*,"
Felt sure that it would pay;
We exceeded our allotment,
And the trip was won that way,
To this great Metropolitan City.

Hurrah! Hurrah! etc.

Another verse, — I must give it :
" Modesty forbids our boasting." The idea ! This will
make you smile, to think of an insurance agent singing of
modesty !

Modesty forbids our boasting;
An excess of delicacy
Refrains us from the mention
(Except 'tween you and me)
That we 're Leaders, Heroes, Giants,
Flowers of the Family,
In this great Metropolitan City.

Hurrah! Hurrah! etc.

Mr. YOUNG. Amen.

Mr. READ. That is what they sing, as the soldiers " sang
the chorus from Atlanta to the sea." And, gentlemen, do
not make a mistake. That music was selected with especial
reference to exciting and arousing the men, — for a good
many of these agents undoubtedly are old soldiers, and they
would remember how they followed Sherman ; and so they

are following the vice-president of the Metropolitan, and
they are swarming through the slums of the cities and
through the homes of the poor, leaving misery in their trail.

Then there is another song :

"Oh! the great trip we took to New York!"

sung to the air "On the Bowery," but I will not stop to
read it.

That is the way the agents are aroused and sent out to
tempt the poor people to give to insurance the money that
ought to be spent for bread for their children.

METHODS OF THE INSURANCE COMPANIES.

I have now told you something about the methods by
which the insurance companies gather in their policies when
they have these men thoroughly roused and at a white-heat,
so to speak, with their gold and their prizes and their songs,
and launch them forth to sweep over the districts of the
poor.

But they have other methods also, and I am now going to
touch upon one of these other methods, because I believe it
my duty to do so, — my duty as a lawyer and a citizen of
this Commonwealth.

I will now refer to the methods of the insurance companies
with regard to the newspapers. And I want to ask the
gentlemen who represent these companies, whether they
think it is right and fair and wholly honorable when we
are trying a case in court,— and you, Mr. Chairman and
gentlemen, with the Legislature, are a court in this matter,—
whether they think it is right and fair and wholly honorable
for the vice-president of the Metropolitan to argue his case
first in this chamber, and then to go to his hotel and rewrite

his argument and publish it in all the newspapers of the city *with conspicuous head-lines*, many of which are *misleading and wholly erroneous*, in such a manner that many people would believe them to be the unbiased expressions of the newspapers, while in fact they are all written by the vice-president himself, and their publication paid for at the rate of *one dollar* a line !

If the head-lines of these articles had been simply " The following is the argument delivered by Vice-President Fiske of the Metropolitan," that would be one thing. But it is a very different thing when the articles bear such head-lines as the following :

" MR. FISKE'S EXHAUSTIVE REPLY TO CHARGES OF PETI-
TIONERS. "

" ATTACK IN REALITY UPON INDUSTRIAL BUSINESS. "

" MR. FISKE MAKES CLEAR THE ANIMUS OF THE ATTACK. "

" ABSURD STARVATION TALES PROVE NONSENSE. "

" MR. FISKE'S CONVINCING ADDRESS. "

Possibly they do things differently in New York, but in Boston I have not observed that it is the custom for men to praise themselves in the public newspapers at one dollar a line, and that is what those printed articles cost, I believe. I have been informed that those printed statements of Mr. Fiske cost $3,000 a day, and they were published on Monday, and again on Wednesday, and again on Friday.

If my figures are correct, the insurance companies have spent $3,000 a day, or $9,000 during the past week upon the newspapers, with the purpose of giving the public and the Legislature to understand that the companies were sweeping everything before them, just as their agents sweep down through the low districts and the poor men's homes.

Here is another paper; they all have different head-lines; this work is very nicely, very skilfully done:

"THE EXPERTS ENDORSE IT."

Look at this, gentlemen:

"STATE LEGISLATION UNIFORMLY IN FAVOR OF THE SYSTEM."

"STARVATION STORIES ABSURD."

"HUMANE SOCIETIES STRONGLY ADVOCATE CHILD INSURANCE."

I say that those statements are not fair, that they are wholly misleading, and if we were trying this case to a jury,—and Governor Long will agree with me,—if we were trying this case to a jury in any court in this State, and statements printed in that manner should be sent to the jury while the jury yet had the matter in hand, the parties so publishing and sending such statements would be guilty of contempt of Court, and the case would be taken from the jury. I remember a case in point in Middlesex County. The case had gone to the jury, when it appeared that a newspaper containing an article written by one of the parties and bearing upon the case had been brought to the attention of the jury, thereupon the Court, upon motion, promptly set the verdict aside.

In this case, suppose the members of the Legislature, as they come from their homes to Boston each morning in the cars, should read these articles; might they not be unconsciously influenced by them?

If we have the good fortune to convince you, gentlemen, this matter will come before the Legislature; and what will the members of the Legislature think, if they chance to read these papers? Let me read from one other paper: —

"Charges Met."

"Infantile Insurance only an Excuse for Attack."

"Mr. Fiske's Able Speech."

This in large type! I charge that those statements and headlines were printed in the newspapers with the deliberate intent and purpose on the part of the companies to unfairly and wrongfully influence the Legislature!

What the press may say about the merits of a case is one thing; but what Mr. Fiske, in his deliberately misleading and self-laudatory articles, publishes about himself is a very different thing, in my opinion. I bring this up, gentlemen of the Committee, because I feel very deeply in this case. I know that we are having a fair trial with you, but human nature is the same the world over. Suppose that you, as members of the Legislature, were not on this committee, and that on Monday last you read some of these papers, and on Wednesday other papers, and on Friday others again, all containing these articles; what would you think? Why, you would think, " There are some philanthropic people up at the State House trying to make out a case." " Here are some able arguments by the insurance companies, splendidly put." " The newspapers all seem to agree that the case of the peti- tioners is wholly without strength or merit and that there is nothing in it." That is what you would think. You would be unconsciously influenced against the petitioners. And that is why I say that this is not a fair way to try this case; and all these articles end with the statement that the news- papers will publish further extracts from Mr. Fiske's address.

Great heavens, gentlemen, if Mr. Fiske is to continue

publishing " further extracts from his Convincing Address," as he has been doing, when will there be an end to it all?

The vice-president spoke in his opening remarks for a whole day; I occupied but one hour with my opening; he spoke for a whole day and for a half day beyond that, and since then he has been deluging the newspapers with his statements, and I suppose that, if you gentlemen report this bill, as I trust that you will, statements of the vice-president will continue to appear in the newspapers,— at one dollar a line,— as long as the Legislature sits, and I cannot help thinking of the words of the poet (with the change of a pronoun),

" For men may come and men may go,
But *he goes* on forever."

If I had the time, I should like to consider further Mr. Fiske's lengthy statement, but he does not meet our position. He discourses on Industrial Insurance and he argues on *death* and child murder. He cites what he calls the most learned work in England upon the subject which we are now investigating, but I have examined that work and I find that it begins with a quotation from Virgil speaking about the *death of infants*, and that the whole book is a book of statistics of *death*. I contend that Mr. Fiske's statement does not touch our case in one single point.

He has just made, however, a statement about some New York letters which I introduced in this hearing a few days ago, and I will, therefore, allude to them at this time to make plain to you the position of Mr. Gerry and Mr. Jenkins, representing the New York Society for the Prevention of Cruelty to Children. The two letters are addressed to Hon. Frank B. Fay.

THE POSITION OF THE NEW YORK SOCIETY.

Mr. Jenkins' letter is dated March 21, 1895, — about ten days ago, — and in it he encloses a copy of the "Proceedings of the State Convention of Societies for the Prevention of Cruelty," held in October last, and states that a committee was then appointed to take into consideration the matter of "Child Insurance" and to report to the Committee on Legislation for Children.

The letter continues: "We are carefully gathering data and facts, and we think that when the matter is presented *it will be somewhat astonishing to the insurance companies.*"

"A bill was introduced in our Legislature two years ago and was defeated, of course, through the insurance companies. There is no doubt that an attempt will be made soon again to regulate this matter by law in New York State, and I am very glad to see that your Society is making the successful fight that it is."

Mr. Jenkins says, "successful," but I suppose I cannot put that word in for a few days yet!

"I will present the matter before President Gerry to-day, and request him to write you a letter, which will be, I think, a denial of all that has been stated and, further, may be, perhaps, a very effective statement for you to read at your hearing. *Personally, I am fully satisfied that ' Child Insurance ' is one of the greatest abuses in our country,* as it has clearly been proven to be by the National Society of England, there.

"Trusting you are well, and that the Society under your guiding hand moves with its usual success,

"I have the honor to remain," etc.

Let me also read you a few lines from President Gerry's letter of March 22, 1895 : —

This *Society is bitterly opposed to the practice of insuring children's lives*, which, iu its judgment, greatly enchances the danger of their not attaining their majority. So far from the Society or myself " being convinced of the value of such insurance," I believe that the same *is pernicious in the extreme, contrary to public policy,* of no *earthly benefit to any of the children themselves* and has a *tendency to promote their premature death.*

I have the honor to remain,

Very sincerely yours,

(Signed) ELBRIDGE T. GERRY,

President, etc.

I do not think there can be much doubt now as to how the New York Society stands with regard to child insurance, in spite of the statements which Mr. Fiske, the vice-president of the Metropolitan, has made.

LAPSED POLICIES — STARTLING FIGURES.

I now ask your attention to the matter of *lapses*. This I am sure you wish to hear about, and, as you know, I have done my best throughout the hearing to obtain from the companies information with regard to the number of lapsed policies, and I had the promise two weeks ago from the Metropolitan and also from the John Hancock that I should have the information, but I have not yet received it, although I have asked for it several times.

I then decided that the insurance companies must have strong reasons for refusing to give the information, and that they were concealing the facts ; so I have now obtained myself the figures in another way, — the *startling* figures as you will see in a moment, — showing how many policies in each of these companies lapsed in 1894, and I will read them to you.

These papers from which I read came from the State House from the insurance commissioners' office, and they have the seal of the insurance department on them. They represent the Exhibit of Industrial Policies which have ceased to be in force by death and *which have lapsed during the year* 1894, in these three companies, respectively: —

In the JOHN HANCOCK COMPANY the number of policies which ceased to be in force by death was 10,154, representing $999,404; the *number* of policies which *lapsed* was *184,638*, representing *$20,878,319*.

In the PRUDENTIAL COMPANY the number of policies which ceased to be in force by death was 1,603, representing $3,834,720; the number of policies which lapsed was *1,345,097*, representing $159,327,057.

In the METROPOLITAN COMPANY the number of policies which ceased to be in force by death, was 57,653,— representing $5,612,408; the number of policies which *lapsed* was 1,637,030, representing $208,295,068.

The figures are indeed *startling*, and they tell better than any words of mine can tell, what becomes of the money of the poor people who take out policies!

These figures, gentlemen, tell something as to how these companies make their millions, and I also think, Mr. Chairman, that they fully explain why these companies have been *unable* (!) (as they have said) to obtain these figures for me.

Mr. Chairman, the counsel for the companies did not *dare* to show these figures to your committee, and they hoped that I would not succeed in getting them ! In this matter also they hoped to mislead your committee and the Legislature ! The figures are *monstrous*, and no further comment is needed !

MORE FIGURES — CLAIMS AND EXPENSES.

I will now give you a few more figures. The claims paid in 1893 in the JOHN HANCOCK COMPANY were $1,116,124.26, and the expenses were $1,749,857.31. Mark you, the expenses are larger than the claims paid. In the PRUDENTIAL COMPANY the claims paid were $2,893,703.33 and the expenses were $4,534,887.96. While in the METROPOLITAN COMPANY the claims paid amounted to $5,535,120.09, and the expenses amounted to $6,636,380.62.

As I said above, no comment is necessary — the figures speak for themselves !

THE COSTLY BUILDINGS OF THE INSURANCE COMPANIES.

Gentlemen of the Committee, I call your particular attention to the fact that throughout the argument which Governor Long has just made he has carefully avoided making any reference whatever to the costly buildings which the insurance companies have erected — and the official report of the stenographers will bear me out in this statement, — Governor Long has kept silent upon this point, hoping that it would escape your notice and my notice. But it has not escaped my notice, and I propose now to refer to it.

Yet, I doubt not that if Governor Long shall print his argument, amended for the Legislature, we shall find that on the very first page he will adroitly allude to these many-storied and capacious buildings just as if in his argument he had anticipated my remarks about them, when, in fact, he has not anticipated my remarks, but he may in print pretend to have done so after reading the stenographic report. If the governor shall do this, it will be because of his anxiety to parry a thrust which he feels is full of danger to his cause.

But if the learned counsel shall do this, we must excuse him, for he is employed to defend grasping corporations in a bad cause.

I do not know whether you have seen the building of the Metropolitan Company in New York, — I will still refer to that company as I shall not have time to speak of all three companies, — but go to Madison Square and look at that palatial edifice, extending from street to street, ten or twelve stories high and built of blocks of marble! Go up, if you please, to the directors' room, where the floor is soft with velvet carpets, and the room is finished in rich red mahogany, while the president and the vice-president sit at their mahogany desks, under the ceiling of pure burnished gold, and there you will find these gentlemen who think what a beautiful thing this child insurance is, and perhaps you and I might think so too, Mr. Chairman, if we could sit in their chairs and receive the salaries which by common repute they are paid. I cannot say with certainty, but I have heard it stated that they each receive $50,000 or $75,000 per annum. But I do know this, that this paper which I hold in my hand, issued by the Metropolitan Company, states one of their ways of *helping the poor* (!), for in it, among other things, I read this item : "A million dollars a month in ten-cent pieces." Think of it! Think of it, gentlemen, "A million dollars a month in ten-cent pieces. The collections of the

Metropolitan last year were not literally as that heading describes them, because a multitude of their collections are five cents each, but for all practical purposes they were, and are correctly stated at a million dollars a month in dimes and nickels."

Now, I call that a sad statement, a pitiful statement. A woman stood here day before yesterday before you, and you saw her; she told you that her husband was a drunkard; that she could earn but fifteen cents an hour; that she had had fifteen policies during about one year on her five little children, and that she had been obliged to "stint her children on their bread" in order to pay the insurance money; and there are some of her policies (tossing a bunch of policies into the air), policies upon which, as long as she was able, by honest toil and out of her slender means, she had paid the premiums. But she had lost them all, for they had *lapsed;* and she had had other policies before those, and they also had lapsed. My feelings are intense in this matter, gentlemen. Her husband, while drunk, had been insured by one of these agents, and her five and ten cent pieces had been sent over to New York to help pay the expenses of this marble palace. And there in that palace sit the officers, except when the president takes his steam yacht to run down to Long Island, or the vice-president saunters up town to his favorite club! What do *they* know about the poor people? You will remember Mr. Fiske's evidence. I asked him if he had ever visited the homes of the poor. He really had never had the time. Ah! Mr. Chairman and gentleman, if I were the president or the vice-president of that company, as I looked up at that magnificent structure, stretching from corner to corner, from street to street, I should see in every block of marble the stony gaze of some poor woman in her misery, or the hungry eyes of some starving child.

CONCLUSION.

Mr. Chairman, I understand that it is one of the functions of the government of the State of Massachusetts to protect the weak, the needy and the unfortunate among her citizens, and the argument of the companies that the State must not prevent a man from taking out insurance upon his own life, if he wishes to do so, does not apply to the case of a man taking out insurance upon the life of his little child, who is not a wage-earner, *and who can receive no possible benefit from such insurance.* And I say to your committee, with all respect, that it is your duty, as I hope it will be your pleasure, to take immediate measures to abolish this cruel child insurance, and so protect young, helpless children in the poor districts of the State. And, in speaking of these little children, our minds involuntarily turn once more to the painful contrast between the palatial buildings of these great corporations and the hovels of the poor, whose little earnings are swallowed up, annually, to meet the corporation expenses. Yes, it is a sad contrast; the poor woman who testified before you, with her drunken husband, her lapsed policies, her lost premiums, and her half-fed little children, and the rich men, sitting in their luxurious offices, drawing their princely salaries — salaries which they could not receive except for this woman, and such as she.

> And what are *her* wages? " A bed of straw,
>   A crust of bread — and rags;
> That shattered roof — and this naked floor,—
>   A table — a broken chair —
> And a wall so blank, my shadow I thank
> For sometimes falling there! "
>   " For the blind and the cripple were there,
>   And the babe that pined for bread."

Oh, gentlemen, if for five minutes I could borrow the power of language of Governor Long, I would paint you such a picture of the misery and poverty and suffering of these poor people that we have been telling you about, that tears would come to your eyes and conviction to your hearts, and before you went out from this chamber to-day you would unanimously vote that the legislation which we ask for shall be granted.

And the last argument that they bring against us is this: that we cannot enact this law, because other States have tried to do so and have failed, and that Great Britain has tried to do so and has failed; how, then, we are asked, can Massachusetts expect to succeed? But I tell you, gentlemen, as I have read the history of the old Commonwealth, it is not in that way that Massachusetts has acted in the past. It has not been her practice to wait for others to show the way, — it has not been her custom to hesitate because others have failed. In 1775 she spoke with no uncertain voice. In 1861, when our great war governor, John A. Andrew, whose son is to-day the president of the society which I have the honor to represent, — when Andrew stood on the steps of this State House, and the volunteers from village and town and city came marching up in battalions and in regiments, eager to strike a blow for the safety and honor of the nation, what said Andrew to those brave men then? Did he say, "Wait and see what other States are doing?" No, sir; he gave them his God-speed and bade them *lead* the way. And in this fight, Mr. Chairman, in this fight for the protection of little children, let Massachusetts take her old place, in the front of the line, — on the right of the line! Do not let her wait for New York, or Pennsylvania, or any other State, or for Great Britain, to show her the way.

Let the old Commonwealth, now as always in the past, *lead*

the way! Let her message be heard in New York "Take courage, Massachusetts has won the fight!" Let the word be sent to Colorado, "Stand firm in the position which you have taken"! Let the good news speed down to Tennessee, "Go on with the brave fight which you are making!" And let the voice of Massachusetts flash under the sea, and carry the tidings to the poor and suffering and oppressed of Great Britain that Massachusetts has taken her accustomed place, and that although others may have failed in this fight, Massachusetts is once more proudly *leading the way* and bidding them to follow; and, Mr. Chairman and gentlemen, I ask you this in the name of the charitable organizations and the charitable men and women throughout this Commonwealth; I ask you this in the name of the parents who are unduly tempted and persuaded to invest their earnings in child insurance; and I ask you this in the name of the tax payers of this State, whose money, given to charity, goes instead to these grasping corporations.

And, lastly, through my lips, let these little hungry-faced children, through all these poor, miserable districts, speak to you, — and they are crying out to you now, "Help us; give us help; we have not enough to eat; we have not enough to wear; can you not, will you not help us? Listen to their pleading, gentlemen, and stamp out forever this cruel, unwise system of child insurance from the Commonwealth of Massachusetts.

www.ingramcontent.com/pod-product-compliance
Lightning Source LLC
Chambersburg PA
CBHW021544270326
41930CB00008B/1359